Design: Art of Design
Recipe Photography: Peter Barry
Jacket and Illustration Artwork: Jane Winton, courtesy
of Bernard Thornton Artists, London
Editors: Jillian Stewart and Kate Cranshaw

CHARTWELL BOOKS
A division of Book Sales, Inc.
POST OFFICE BOX 7100
114 Northfield Avenue
Edison, N.J. 08818-7100

CLB 3520
© 1995 CLB Publishing,
Godalming, Surrey, England.
Printed and bound in Singapore
ISBN 0-7858-0230-4

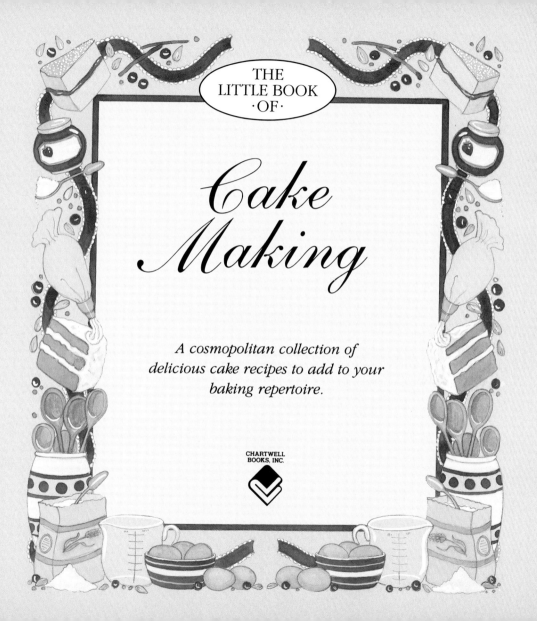

THE LITTLE BOOK ·OF·

Cake Making

A cosmopolitan collection of delicious cake recipes to add to your baking repertoire.

CHARTWELL
BOOKS, INC.

Introduction

There is something of great social significance about cakes and cake making. Cakes are about occasions; they are to do with entertaining, enjoyment, indulgence. Cakes are about the good things in life. There are cakes for birthdays, for weddings, for christenings, and for anniversaries. There are cakes for Christmas and Easter and Halloween. There are cakes for the opening of plays, films and buildings, and for the launching of ships. And there are cakes simply to accompany coffee. A cake is always an indication of goodwill, of wanting to share, and of wanting to be sociable -- and of course there is often an element of wanting to impress!

Cakes do not have to be ornate, although there is a great trend nowadays to decorate a cake into any one of a fantastic number of themes: fairytales, skating boots, cartoon characters for children's birthday parties, wedding cakes with tiny iced slippers representing the giving away of the bride. All these are fine, and particularly magnificent to look at, but often the energy and ingenuity spent on the decoration is greater than that devoted to the cake mixture. Such cakes can be too good to cut, and not good enough to eat!

The recipes here are about delicious ingredients and wholesome and mouthwatering tastes to be shared with friends and relations. Coffee breaks and tea-time are ideal times at

which to indulge in cake eating. These are both rather anachronistic in these modern times of calorie counting and weight watching, but life would be dull indeed if we did not give in to culinary temptations from time to time. It is surely far better to slice into a delicious homemade cake as a special treat than to resort, in a gnawing, hungry moment, to a clutch of candy bars. The secret is to plan your treats in advance, bake the chosen cake, and then to bring it out with a flourish to delight your family and friends at the time of need.

Cake making techniques and methods vary tremendously and, indeed, are also of social significance. A cake mixture can be rushed, literally in a minute or two, from food processor bowl into the oven. Modern pressures of work and family commitments, all to be squeezed into a day that is never long enough, are such that a cake is frequently thrown together in this way. The food processor's greatest use is probably for cake making. It is difficult, however, not to feel a certain nostalgia for those days when the only cake-making utensils were the wooden spoon and the stoneware mixing bowl. Of course, there are still plenty of people who make cakes in the traditional way. It is all a matter of personal preference, and how much time you have on your hands. It is nice, though, to think that a handmade cake has a little extra love and sympathy stirred into it.

Coconut Layer Cake

SERVES 6

The addition of coconut to this delicious cake helps keep it moist.

PREPARATION: 20 mins
COOKING: 25 mins

1 cup butter
2 cups sugar
3 eggs, separated
3 cups all-purpose flour
2 tsps baking powder
1 cup coconut milk
⅔ cups freshly-grated coconut
Seedless raspberry jelly

1. Cream together the butter and sugar in a mixing bowl until pale and fluffy. Beat in the egg yolks one by one, beating well after each addition.

2. Sift together the flour and the baking powder and fold into the butter mixture alternately with the coconut milk, stirring after each addition until the mixture is smooth.

3. Stir in two-thirds of the grated coconut. Whisk the egg whites until stiff then fold them gently into the cake mixture.

4. Divide the mixture between three greased shallow cake pans and bake in an oven preheated to 350°F about 25 minutes, or until springy to the touch. Turn out onto a wire rack to cool.

5. To assemble the cake, sandwich the layers together with the raspberry jelly. Spread another layer of jelly over the top of the cake and sprinkle with the remaining coconut.

Almond Layer Cake

MAKES ONE 8-INCH ROUND CAKE

Definitely not for the diet conscious, but delicious for those wishing to sin.

PREPARATION: 40 mins
COOKING: 35 mins

¼ cup dry white breadcrumbs
½ cup milk
2 tbsps rum
⅓ cup unsalted butter or margarine
3 tbsps superfine sugar
6 eggs, separated
3 tbsps roasted almonds, ground
2½ cups heavy cream
2 tbsps powdered sugar
2 tbsps roasted almonds, finely chopped
Whole blanched almonds, lightly toasted

---

1. Put the breadcrumbs into a large bowl and pour the milk and half of the rum over them. Leave until the liquid has been completely absorbed.

2. Beat the butter in a large bowl until soft. Gradually add the sugar, mixing until light and fluffy. Beat in the egg yolks, one at a time, mixing well. Fold in the breadcrumbs.

3. Whisk the egg whites until stiff, but not dry. Fold into the mixture with the ground almonds.

Step 3 Beat the egg yolks, one at a time, into the butter and sugar mixture, mixing well to prevent curdling.

4. Divide the cake mixture equally between 3 × 8-inch round cake pans; all greased, floured and lined. Bake in an oven preheated to 350°F, for 30-35 minutes, until well risen and golden. Cool briefly before turning onto a wire rack.

5. Whip the cream until stiff, then beat in the powdered sugar and remaining rum. Reserve one third of the cream and fold the finely-chopped almonds into the rest.

6. Sandwich the cake layers together with the almond cream, then spread the plain cream over the top, reserving some for piping. Decorate with the toasted whole almonds. Pipe whorls of cream around the edge.

Guinness Cake

MAKES ONE 9-INCH CAKE

Guinness adds a lovely flavor to this rich fruit cake.

PREPARATION: 25 mins
COOKING: 2 hrs

1 cup butter or margarine
1 cup brown sugar
1½ cups Guinness
1 cup raisins
1 cup currants
1 cup sultanas
½ cup chopped candied peels
5 cups all-purpose flour
1 tsp allspice
1 tsp nutmeg
½ tsp baking soda
3 eggs, beaten

1. Place the butter, sugar, and the Guinness in a saucepan and bring slowly to the boil, stirring constantly until the sugar and butter have melted.

2. Mix in the dried fruits and candied peel and bring the mixture back to the boil, then simmer 5 minutes. Remove from the heat and cool thoroughly.

3. Sift the flour, spices, and baking soda into a large mixing bowl. Stir in the cooled fruit mixture and add the beaten eggs.

4. Turn into a greased and lined deep 9-inch cake pan and bake in the center of an oven preheated to 325°F 2 hours or until a skewer inserted in the center comes out clean. When done, cool in the pan before removing to a cake rack.

Saffron Babas

MAKES 2 CAKES

This is a traditional Polish Easter cake. Cooks spoke in whispers when these cakes were cooling since loud noise was believed to damage the delicate texture!

PREPARATION: 2 hrs
COOKING: 40-50 mins

10½ cups all-purpose flour
2 cups lukewarm milk
3 tbsps fresh yeast
¾ cup sugar
4 eggs plus 4 yolks
Grated rind of 1 lemon
3 tbsps brandy
Pinch powdered saffron
Pinch salt
¾ cup melted butter, slightly cooled
½ cup raisins
2 tbsps chopped mixed candied peel

Step 4 Leave the dough to rise a second time in the cake pans until completely filled.

1. First prepare a "sponge." Pour 2½ cups of the sifted flour into a bowl. Make a well in the center. Combine the milk and yeast and pour into in the center of the flour. Mix with a wooden spoon and cover with plastic wrap.

2. Leave in a warm place about 1 hour, until the sponge doubles in bulk and the top becomes bubbly and spongy.

3. Combine the sugar together with the eggs and egg yolks, lemon rind, brandy, and saffron. Mix with the flour mixture and add the remaining flour and salt. Knead by hand about 30 minutes in the bowl or on a well-floured surface.

4. Place the dough back in the bowl and add the butter, raisins, and peel. Knead until it is smooth and elastic and does not stick to the sides of the bowl. Divide in 2 equal portions. Butter two 10-inch round cake pans very thickly and put the dough in them, patting it out evenly. Cover each with lightly-oiled plastic wrap and put in a warm place to rise until the pans are filled.

5. Bake in an oven preheated to 400°F about 40-50 minutes, or until a toothpick inserted into the center of each comes out clean. Leave to cool in the pans about 10-14 minutes and then remove to a cooling rack. Sprinkle with sugar or sprinkle with frosting.

Poppyseed Cake

SERVES 6-8

This is the Christmas version of an ever-popular Polish cake.

PREPARATION: 1 hr
COOKING: 45-50 mins

Dough
⅓ cup butter or margarine
⅓ cup sugar
1 egg
3-4 tbsps lukewarm milk
1½ tbsps dry yeast
3 cups all-purpose flour

Filling
1 cup milk
½ cup poppyseeds
3 tbsps butter or margarine
5 tbsps liquid honey
2 tbsps ground walnuts
3 tbsps raisins
1 tbsp finely chopped candied peel
1 egg
2 tbsps sugar
3 tbsps brandy

1. To prepare the dough, cream the butter with the sugar until light and fluffy, and gradually add the egg, beating in well. Add a pinch of salt. Dissolve the yeast in the milk and add to the other ingredients. Sift in the flour and mix to a dough. Knead well until smooth and elastic.

2. To test if the dough has been sufficiently kneaded, press lightly – if it springs back fairly quickly, it is ready to leave to rise.

3. Place the dough in a lightly-greased bowl, cover with a damp cloth, and leave in a warm place about 1 hour, or until doubled in bulk.

4. For the filling, boil the milk then add the poppyseeds. Cook over low heat about 30 minutes, stirring frequently. Drain the seeds well and grind to a paste in a liquidizer.

5. Melt the butter and add the honey, walnuts, raisins, and candied peel. Add the poppyseed paste and cook about 15 minutes, stirring frequently over moderate heat.

6. Beat the egg with the sugar until light and fluffy and add to the poppyseed mixture. Cook over gentle heat, stirring constantly to thicken. Add the brandy, and set aside.

7. When the dough has doubled in bulk, punch it back and knead a further 2-5 minutes. Roll out thinly on a floured surface, shaping it into a rectangle. Spread the filling evenly over it and roll up tightly as for a jellyroll, pressing the ends together to seal. Place on a lightly buttered baking tray curving into a horseshoe shape. Bake in an oven preheated to 375°F 45-50 minutes, or until golden-brown. Serve plain or with frosting.

Irish Coffee Cake

SERVES 8

This is a delicious cake flavored with Irish whiskey and covered with whipped cream.

PREPARATION: 30 mins
COOKING: 35-40 mins

½ cup butter or margarine
½ cup superfine sugar
2 eggs
1 cup all-purpose flour
1 tsp baking powder
2 tsps instant coffee dissolved in 2 tbsps hot
    water

Sirup
½ cup sugar
¾ cup strong black coffee
3 tbsps Irish whiskey

Topping
⅔ cup whipping cream
2 tbsps powdered sugar
1 tbsp Irish whiskey
Whole hazelnuts or pecans

---

1. In a bowl, cream the butter and sugar until light and fluffy, then add the eggs one at a time, beating in well.

2. Sift the flour and baking powder together and fold two-thirds of it into the creamed mixture, using a metal spoon. Add the dissolved coffee and mix in well. Fold in the remainder of the flour.

3. Place in a greased and floured 8-inch tube pan and bake in an oven preheated to 350°F 35-40 minutes, or until a skewer comes out clean when inserted in the middle. Turn out onto a wire rack to cool.

4. To make the sirup, heat the sugar in the coffee until dissolved then boil rapidly 1 minute. Remove from the heat and beat in the whiskey.

5. Return the cooled cake to the well-washed pan and pour the sirup over it. Leave it to soak for several hours.

6. Beat the cream with the powdered sugar and whiskey. Turn the cake out onto a serving platter and decorate with the cream and whole nuts. Chill before serving.

Sirup Cake

SERVES 8

Rather like gingerbread, this cake can be served with coffee, or warm with cream as a dessert.

PREPARATION: 20 mins
COOKING: 45 mins

1 cup white vegetable shortening
1 cup blackstrap molasses
3 eggs, beaten
3 cups all-purpose flour
Pinch salt
1 tbsp baking powder
1 tsp cinnamon
¼ tsp ground nutmeg
Pinch ground cloves
4 tbsps chopped nuts
4 tbsps raisins

1. Cream the shortening until light and fluffy.

Step 1 Cream the shortening until light and fluffy. Beat in the treacle with an electric mixer.

Step 2 Sift in the dry ingredients and combine by hand.

Add the molasses and beat with an electric mixer. Add the eggs one at a time, beating well in between each addition.

2. Sift the flour together with a pinch of salt, the baking powder, and spices. Fold into the treacle mixture.

3. Stir in the nuts and raisins and pour the mixture into a lightly-greased 9 × 13 inch cake pan or baking dish.

4. Bake in an oven preheated to 375°F about 45 minutes, or until a toothpick inserted into the center of the cake comes out clean. Allow to cool and cut into squares to serve.

Victoria Sandwich Cake

SERVES 6-8

This is the classic cake to serve for English afternoon tea, but it tastes equally good with coffee.

PREPARATION: 20 mins
COOKING: 25 mins

½ cup butter or margarine
½ cup superfine sugar
2 large eggs
Few drops vanilla extract
1 cup self-rising flour, sifted

To finish
Jam, whipped cream and sifted powdered
   sugar

---

1. In a medium-sized mixing bowl, cream together the butter and sugar until light and fluffy. Beat in the eggs one at a time and the vanilla extract.

2. With a metal spoon, gently fold in the sifted flour. When it is all incorporated, divide the mixture equally between two greased and lined 7-inch shallow cake pans, leveling off the surface.

3. Bake in the center of an oven preheated to 350°F about 25 minutes. Test by pressing your finger gently onto the sponge; it should feel springy and leave no impression when the cake is done.

4. Leave to cool for a minute in the pans, then turn out onto wire cooling racks and carefully peel off the parchment or nonstick baking paper.

5. When cold, sandwich together with jam and whipped cream, and dust the top with sifted powdered sugar.

23

Christmas Cake

MAKES ONE 9-INCH SQUARE CAKE

Although this fruit cake is made without eggs and sugar, it is still rich and moist.

PREPARATION: 40 mins
COOKING: 3¼-3½ hrs

½ cup clear honey
¾ cup safflower or sunflower oil
⅓ cup soya flour
1¼ cups water
1 tbsp rum or 1 tsp rum extract
Grated rind and juice of 1 orange
Grated rind and juice of 1 lemon
2 tbsps flaked almonds
3 dried figs, chopped
6 dried dates, chopped
4 dried apricots, chopped
2 cups wholewheat flour
1 tbsps double-acting baking powder
Pinch salt
2 tsps mixed spice
1 cup currants
1 cup golden raisins
1 cup raisins

---

1. Cream the honey and the oil.

2. Mix the soya flour with the water and gradually add to the oil and honey mixture, beating well.

3. Beat in the rum, and the grated rind and juice of the orange and lemon. Add the almonds, figs, dates, and apricots.

4. Mix the wholewheat flour and baking powder with the salt and spice and mix together the currants, golden raisins, and raisins.

5. Stir half the flour and half the raisin mixture into the soya cream, then stir in the remainder. Spoon into a greased and lined deep 9-inch square cake pan.

6. Cover with two or three layers of brown wrapping paper and bake in an oven preheated to 325°F 3¼-3½ hours, or until a skewer inserted into the center comes out clean.

7. Cool 10 minutes in the pan, then unmold onto a wire rack to cool completely. Store 3-4 weeks in an airtight container wrapped in wax or parchment paper, before cutting.

25

Kugelhopf

SERVES 8

This Continental yeasted cake is an ideal coffee cake.

PREPARATION: 40 mins, plus 2 hrs proving
COOKING: 45 mins

4½ cups all-purpose flour
1 cup warm milk
4 tsps fresh yeast
2 tbsps plum liqueur or brandy
⅓ cup raisins
¼ tsp salt
2 eggs
½ cup sugar
¾ cup butter, softened
5 tbsps slivered almonds

---

1. Mix together 5 tbsps of the flour with half of the warm milk and all the yeast and leave for 1

Step 2 Knead the dough in the bowl, using your hands, for at least 5 minutes.

Step 4 When the dough has tripled in volume, mix in the raisins and almonds.

hour in a warm place. Pour the liqueur or brandy over the raisins and leave to soak.

2. Mix the salt, eggs, sugar, and remaining milk into the rest of the flour. Knead the dough at least 5 minutes in the bowl with your hands.

3. Knead in the softened butter and the yeast mixture until well mixed, then set the dough aside in a warm place for 1 hour, or until tripled in volume.

4. When the dough has risen sufficiently, mix in the raisins and almonds. Place in a greased kugelhopf mold or bundt pan and bake in an oven preheated to 350°F 45 minutes. Allow to rest in the pan for 15 minutes before unmolding.

Sour Cream Cake

SERVES 8-10

This delicious cake may be flavored with more or less cinnamon, as preferred.

PREPARATION: 20 mins
COOKING: 40 mins

½ cup butter
1 cup sugar
2 eggs
⅔ cup sour cream
1 tsp baking soda
1½ cups all-purpose flour
1½ tsps baking powder
1 tsp vanilla extract

Topping
3 tbsps brown sugar
2 tbsps chopped mixed nuts
2 tsps cinnamon

---

1. In a large bowl, cream together the butter and sugar, until light and fluffy.

2. Beat in the eggs and sour cream mixed with the baking soda. Blend well.

3. Sift together the flour and baking powder and fold in gently using a metal spoon. Add the vanilla.

4. Mix all the topping ingredients together. Pour half of the cake mixture into a greased 9-inch tube pan and sprinkle with half the topping.

5. Pour in the remaining mixture and sprinkle with the rest of the topping.

6. Bake in an oven preheated to 350°F 40 minutes, or until risen and springy to the touch.

Carrot Cake with Apricot Filling

SERVES 6-8

This tasty cake will freeze well for up to 2 months.

PREPARATION: 20 mins
COOKING: 45-50 mins

---

8 dried apricots
⅔ cup butter or margarine
⅔ cup brown sugar
2 eggs, separated
1 cup all-purpose flour
1 tsp baking powder
1 cup peeled and finely grated carrots
¼ cup golden raisins
¼ cup walnuts, finely chopped
2 tsps grated lemon rind
½ tsp ground cinnamon

---

1. Soak the apricots in water overnight, drain and liquidize until smooth.

2. Beat the butter and sugar together until pale and creamy.

3. Whisk the egg yolks and beat into the butter and sugar.

4. Sift the flour and baking powder and fold into the mixture.

5. Fold in the rest of the ingredients except the egg whites.

6. Whisk the egg whites until they form soft peaks, and fold into the mixture.

7. Place the mixture in a greased 7-inch round springform pan. Bake in an oven preheated to 350°F 45-50 minutes.

8. Cool in the pan 10 minutes and then unmold onto a wire rack.

9. When completely cooled, slice in half and sandwich together with the apricot sauce.

Praline Sponge Cake

SERVES 4

This extravagant dessert cake is well worth its slightly time-consuming assembly and will earn you many compliments! Praline can be bought from candy shops.

PREPARATION: 1 hr 30 mins
COOKING: 25 mins

4 eggs
¾ cup sugar
1½ cups all-purpose flour, sifted
2 tbsps melted butter

Praline cream filling
1 tbsp unflavored gelatin
5½ tbsps sugar
3 egg yolks
4 tsps all-purpose flour
2 cups milk
8 tbsps praline
¾ cup heavy cream
Extra whipped cream and crushed praline to decorate

Step 1 Beat until the mixture forms ribbons.

1. In a bowl, beat the eggs and sugar over a pan of simmering water until the mixture is pale and thick. Remove the bowl, and continue to beat until cooled, and the mixture forms ribbons when dropped from a whisk.

2. Gently fold in the flour and the melted butter, then three quarters-fill a greased-and-floured deep cake pan. Bake in an oven preheated to 325°F 25 minutes, or until springy to the touch. Turn out onto a wire rack and allow to cool, then slice crosswise into four layers.

3. To make the filling, dissolve the gelatin in a little hot water. Mix the sugar, egg yolks, and flour together. Bring the milk to the boil with all but 2 tbsps of the praline, stirring to dissolve. Pour over the egg yolk mixture, and mix together well. Return to the pan and stir over low heat until thickened. Stir in the gelatin, then allow to cool 15 minutes, stirring occasionally.

4. Whip the cream until stiff, then fold it gently but thoroughly into the filling. Crush the reserved 2 tbsps praline with a rolling-pin and fold it into the filling.

5. Cover the sponge layers with filling. Use a metal spatula to spread the last fourth of filling over the top and sides of the cake. Chill 2 hours before serving, then decorate with extra whipped cream and crushed praline.

Redcurrant Griestorte

SERVES 6

This light, delicious cake would taste equally good if filled with other fruit such as raspberries or blueberries.

PREPARATION: 20 mins
COOKING: 30 mins

Small amount of caster sugar and flour
3 large eggs, separated
⅔ cup superfine sugar
Grated rind and juice of 1 lemon
1 tbsp ground almonds
4 tbsps fine farina or cornmeal
½ cup heavy cream
1 tbsp milk
½ cup redcurrants
Powdered sugar

1. Line an 8 × 12 inch jellyroll pan with nonstick baking paper, making a collar that stands up above the rim. Butter the paper and sprinkle with a little superfine sugar, and a dusting of flour.

2. In a bowl, whisk the egg yolks with the sugar until pale, thick, and creamy. Whisk in the lemon juice. Combine ground almonds, farina or cornmeal, and lemon rind, and carefully stir into the mixture.

3. Whisk the egg whites until stiff, then fold the egg yolk mixture gently through the egg whites. Turn into the prepared pan. Bake in an oven preheated to 350°F about 30 minutes or until risen, pale golden brown, and springy to the touch.

4. Turn out carefully onto a sheet of nonstick baking paper dusted with superfine sugar. Trim the edges if necessary, then roll up loosely with some nonstick baking paper inside, and leave to cool on a wire rack.

5. Whisk together the cream and milk until fairly stiff. Unroll the cake, spread with the cream, and sprinkle with the redcurrants, reserving some for decoration. Roll up, dust with powdered sugar, and decorate with the reserved fruits.

Pineapple Upside-Down Cake

SERVES 6

This old favorite makes an ideal dessert on a cold winter's day.

PREPARATION: 30 mins
COOKING: 45 mins

2 large eggs
1 cup butter or margarine
½ cup superfine sugar
¾ cup self-rising flour
2 tbsps ground almonds
2 tbsps milk
½ tsp vanilla extract
Few drops almond extract

Topping
Small can pineapple rings, drained and halved
2 tbsps butter
1 tbsp soft brown sugar
2-4 tbsps candied cherries, halved

1. Cream the butter and sugar until light and fluffy. Beat the eggs lightly and gradually add to the creamed mixture together with the extracts.

2. Sift the flour, stir in the ground almonds and fold into the mixture, using a metal tablespoon. Add the milk to make a soft mixture.

3. Melt the butter for the topping in an 8-inch square cake pan or a 7-inch round pan and use to grease the sides.

4. Sprinkle the brown sugar over the melted butter. Arrange the pineapple halves on the sugared base and decorate with the cherries.

5. Carefully spread the cake mixture over the fruits. Bake in an oven preheated to 375°F 45 minutes. Remove from the oven, loosen the sides with a knife, and turn out onto a warmed platter.

6. Serve with cream or half-and-half, or make a sauce using the pineapple juice thickened with 2 tsps of cornstarch, boiled 2-3 minutes, and sweetened to taste.

Pound Cake

This is a classic plain sand cake that complements fruit salads to perfection, and is also a welcome addition at coffee time.

PREPARATION: 20 mins
COOKING: 45 mins

1½ cups softened unsalted butter
1½ cups superfine sugar
5 eggs
½ tsp vanilla extract, or 2 tsps orangeflower
 water
2 tsps baking powder
3 cups all-purpose flour

---

1. In a large mixing bowl cream together the butter and sugar until light and fluffy.

Step 3 Fold in the sifted flour and baking powder.

Step 3 Spoon the mixture into a nonstick loaf pan.

2. Beat in the eggs one at a time, together with the vanilla or orangeflower water. Beat well between each addition, to ensure that the egg is fully incorporated before adding more; this will prevent the mixture from curdling.

3. Sift the baking powder with the flour then fold into the mixture, which should be thick and creamy. Spoon the cake mixture into either a nonstick or a greased and lined loaf pan.

4. Bake in an oven preheated to 350°F about 45 minutes, or until a toothpick inserted in the center of the cake comes out clean. Turn out onto a wire rack to cool.

Apple Cake

SERVES 8

Serve this delicious cake warm with applesauce and cream or half-and-half.

PREPARATION: 20 mins
COOKING: 45 mins

---

1 tsp cinnamon
1½ cups self-rising flour
¾ cup butter or margarine
¾ cup superfine sugar
3 eggs
2 tbsps milk
2-3 dessert apples, peeled, cored, and thinly
  sliced

---

1. Add the cinnamon to the flour and sift into a bowl. Cream the butter and sugar until pale and fluffy.

2. Beat in the eggs one at a time, adding 1 tbsp of the flour after each egg is incorporated. Fold in two-thirds of the remaining flour, then stir in the milk, before folding in the last of the flour.

3. Grease an 11 × 8½-inch ovenproof dish or mold. Spread half the mixture in the dish, distribute the apple slices over it and cover with the rest of the mixture.

4. Bake in an oven preheated to 350°F 15 minutes, then reduce heat to 325°F, and continue baking 30 minutes until golden-brown and firm to the touch.

Lemon Cake

SERVES 6-8

This cake will taste just as good if orange is substituted for the lemon.

PREPARATION: 15 mins
COOKING: 45 mins

½ cup butter
1 cup sugar
1 lemon
2 eggs, separated
2 cups all-purpose flour
1½ tsps baking powder
½ cup milk
4 tbsps lemon cheese (optional)
4 tbsps powdered sugar (optional)

---

1. Cream the butter and sugar until pale and fluffy. Grate the lemon rind and beat in along with 2 tsps of the juice. Beat in the egg yolks one at a time.

2. Sift the flour and the baking powder, and add to the butter mixture in batches, alternately with the milk. Beat well after each addition to obtain a smooth mixture.

3. Whisk the egg whites until stiff and fold them gently into the cake mixture.

4. Turn the batter into a greased cake pan, and bake 45 minutes in an oven preheated to 350°F, or until springy to the touch. Turn out onto a cake rack and leave to cool.

5. The cake can be split, and sandwiched together with lemon cheese and dusted with powdered sugar on the top.

Index